The **Sophia Day**™ Creative Team-
Kayla Pearson, Timothy Zowada,
Stephanie Strouse, Megan Johnson, Mel Sauder

Designed by Stephanie Strouse

Published and Distributed by MVP Kids Media, LLC
Mesa, Arizona, USA
Printed by RR Donnelley Asia Printing Solutions, Ltd
Dongguan City, Guangdong Province, China
DOM Sept 2018, Job # 03-005-01

Becoming *a Hero*
& Overcoming **Bullying**™

REAL
mvpkids®

STOP BULLYING

S.T.A.N.D.
a 3-part series

STAND Together
Against Bullying

SOPHIA DAY®

Written by Kayla Pearson   Illustrated by Timothy Zowada

TABLE OF CONTENTS

STORY	PAGE

Lucas' Hiking Surprise

"Time for a break, Soaring Explorers!" said Lucas' group leader.

Lucas stopped for a drink of water. He loved being in nature.

The leader gave the group time to explore the area. Some kids who often picked on a boy named Wesley walked up to Lucas.

"Hey Lucas! You should come with us. We are staying away from Wesley. He's so annoying," said one of them.

Lucas looked over at Wesley, who was alone.

There were times when Wesley did things that were a *little* unusual, but Lucas didn't think he should be left out.

This sounded a lot like *bullying*. Lucas remembered what the group leader said about how to **STAND** against bullying.

"Remember to:

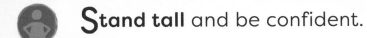

Stand tall and be confident.

Tell an adult if you run into trouble.

Act bravely and walk away if you need to.

Notice what is going on around you.

Display kindness to others."

Lucas **kindly** replied, "No thanks. I think I will go see if Wesley has found anything interesting." Lucas **walked away**.

"No, I just wanted to see if you found anything," Lucas answered.

"Oh. Um. I think I have, but I can't lift this log," said Wesley as he pointed at a stone.

Lucas saw part of a fossil in the rock underneath the log. "Whoa! That looks neat," said Lucas.

The boys tried to lift the log but it was too heavy.

Lucas ran to the others. "Wesley found something, but we need your help!" Lucas gathered others to help lift the log.

When everyone worked together to help Wesley, they were able to lift the heavy log to grab the fossil.

"Wow! Wesley found a trilobite fossil! These creatures lived a long time ago. Their fossils are very rare to find. Way to go Wesley!"

After looking at the fossil,
Wesley walked up to Lucas.

"Thanks for being my friend when nobody else would," said Wesley.

"I'm happy to be your friend," replied Lucas.

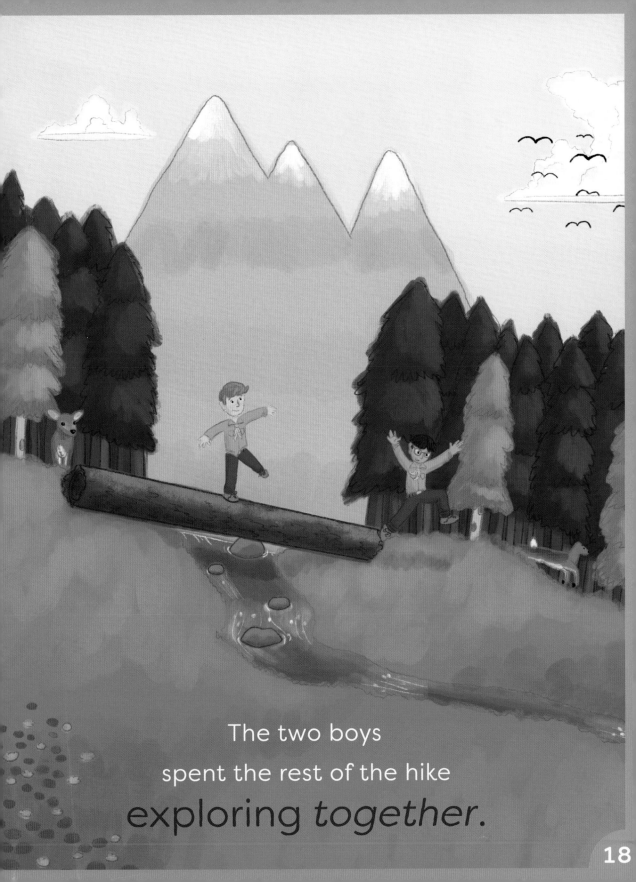

The two boys
spent the rest of the hike
exploring together.

THINK & TALK ABOUT IT

Lucas' Hiking Surprise

Discuss the story...

1. What was Lucas doing in the woods?

2. Why did Lucas walk away from the boys who didn't want to play with Wesley?

3. How did Lucas display kindness to the boys who were bullying Wesley?

4. How did Lucas display kindness to Wesley?

5. What ways did Lucas **STAND** against bullying?

 Stand Confident   Tell an Adult   Act Bravely & Walk Away   Notice Surroundings   Display Kindness

*For additional tips and reference information, visit **www.realMVPkids.com**.*

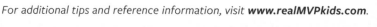

Discuss how to apply the story...

1. What are some different ways kids bully other kids?

2. How do you feel when you see someone being bullied?

3. How do you feel when someone is kind to you?

4. Do you know kids who feel left out? What are some ways you can be their friend?

5. Do you know kids who are mean to others? What are some ways you can be their friend?

FOR PARENTS & MENTORS: *Bullying can take different forms. People often recognize physical bullying but don't know that bullying can be verbal (teasing), mental (threatening or shaming) or social (rumors or leaving someone out). To prepare your children to notice bullying situations, talk with them about ways that children might bully others. Provide examples of how to avoid participating in those behaviors, such as, "During lunch, if you witness someone being left out intentionally, try sitting with them when others won't.*

In this world where so many people are hurting, kindness is a powerful tool. Talk with your child about ways they can display kindness to others. Encourage them to befriend those who might not have many friends and treat everyone with respect. Even teaching kids how to stand up in a respectful way to other kids who are bullying can have a profound effect on this bullying epidemic.

Faith's Drama Practice

Faith enjoyed being in drama club. She loved **singing** and **dancing**. Someday she wanted to perform in front of an audience!

Each practice they started with a warm-up game. "Today we're going to play the animal game!" said Miss Gomez, Faith's drama teacher.

"One, two, here we go!

Slump around like a sad elephant.

Jump up and down like a happy puppy.

Roar really loud like an angry dragon.

Flutter your wings like a **thankful** turkey.

Jump back like a **scared** rabbit.

Stand tall like a **brave** horse."

"Great job, class! Now let's practice using our strongest, bravest voice for when we are on stage. One of you will pretend to be an angry dragon picking on the scared rabbit.

Then the brave horse will come in to yell, 'Stop right there!' and save the rabbit. I want you to yell in your loudest, strongest, bravest voice so I can hear you in the back of the theater."

Each child took turns playing
the different animals.

Faith didn't like
playing the part
of the angry
dragon.

She didn't like
playing the scared
rabbit either.

Her favorite part was being the horse, because she liked being the hero.

"That's all we have time for today! Don't forget to start practicing your lines for the end of the year performance."

After practice, Faith and Olivia were playing in the hallway waiting for their parents to pick them up.

All of a sudden, they **noticed** some voices in the next hallway. It sounded like **someone was** in trouble. They peeked around the corner.

"*Hey! Leave me alone!*"
Two kids were intimidating someone.
Faith could tell they were not going to stop.

"Olivia, *quick*! Go get Miss Gomez."

Olivia ran back to the drama room.

Faith remembered the brave horse in her play. She **stood tall** and yelled in her strongest, bravest voice, *"Stop right there!"* This surprised the kids. They froze and looked around. *"Leave him alone!"* Faith yelled, again in her strongest, loudest, bravest voice.

The two kids started to walk toward Faith. By this time, Miss Gomez had arrived.

The kids tried to run away, but Miss Gomez caught them. She took them to the principal's office.

Faith and Olivia displayed kindness by helping pick up the boy's things.

When Miss Gomez came back, Faith told her, "I used what you taught us in drama to stop them!"

"Great job Faith and Olivia for STANDing together against bullying."

THINK & TALK ABOUT IT

Faith's Drama Practice

Discuss the story...

1. Which animal did Faith like being the most?

2. What happened when Faith and Olivia were playing in the hallway?

3. What was the first thing Faith did when she noticed someone being bullied?

4. How did Faith act bravely?

5. What ways did Faith and Olivia **STAND** together against bullying?

 Stand Confident

 Tell an Adult

 Act Bravely & Walk Away

 Notice Surroundings

 Display Kindness

Discuss how to apply the story...

1. Which animal from the animal game would you want to act like?

2. How do you think a child being bullied feels? How do you think a child who bullies others feels?

3. Why is it important to notice what is going on around you?

4. What would you do if you saw someone being bullied?

5. Why do you think it is important to tell an adult when you see someone being bullied?

FOR PARENTS & MENTORS: *Empathy, the ability to understand what others are feeling, is an important life skill and can help when dealing with bullying behaviors. Bullying affects not only the victim and the bully, but also the bystanders as well, and it can affect all involved in different ways. Children who are bullied may feel fear, sadness, loneliness, helplessness or anger. Children who bully others may feel anger, insecurity, shame or loneliness. Children who witness bullying may feel fear, anxiety, helplessness or guilt. Talking through these different emotions can help children be more understanding and inclusive of others. Also, role-playing a bullying situation can help build the confidence needed to stand against bullying.*

For additional tips and reference information, visit **www.realMVPkids.com**.

Leo's Trip to the Science Museum

"I can't wait to see the new, fast-car exhibit!" Leo said as he walked into the science museum. Today was their class field trip.

On the way to the fast-car exhibit, Leo's group went to the **building blocks exhibit.** As they walked into the room, a man and woman at the front of the room were showing everyone how the ancient Romans built arches.

44

"You see, in order for the stone blocks to make an arch, they have to lean on each other. They can't hold very much on their own, but together they can support each other."

After the presentation, Leo's group started working together to build an arch. The blocks reminded Leo of how his friends supported him. With the help of each other, Leo's group was able to do more than they could on their own.

While they were working, Leo **noticed** a boy from their class bossing around another kid. Charlie was known for being mean to others. He was always calling people names and threatening them.

1 = I   6 = VI

2 = II   7 = VII

3 = III   = VIII

= IX

V

He had even made fun of Leo a
couple of times. Leo remembered how
he *wished* someone
had stood up for him.

Leo knew he had to **do something,** but didn't think he could do it on his own. He turned to his group and **asked for their help.**

"I don't know. Charlie can be really mean. *What if he hurts us?*" said Blake.

"I know he's scary, but we'll support each other. If we all **STAND** **tall together** I think we can get him to stop," said Leo. They agreed and walked over to Charlie and the boy.

"Charlie, you should **stop picking on him**," said Ezekiel.

"It bugs us when you pick on others. We wish you would be kind," said Frankie.

At first Charlie wouldn't stop, but they were able to **S**TAN**D** together.

Finally they were able to get him to walk away.

"Are you all right?"

Leo asked the boy. The boy nodded his head.

"What's your name?"   "My name is Elan,"
the boy answered.

Leo and his friends displayed kindness to Elan by inviting him to join their group for the rest of the day.

They **told their chaperone** about Charlie, so he could get the help he needed to stop bullying.

Then they each got to go to their favorite exhibits.

Leo liked knowing he had friends who could count on each other.

THINK & TALK ABOUT IT

Leo's Trip to the Museum

Discuss the story...

1. Where did Leo go for his class field trip?

2. What did Leo's group learn about in the building blocks exhibit?

3. What did Leo notice while they were working?

4. How did Leo's friends support him?

5. What ways did Leo and his friends **STAND** together against bullying?

 **Stand Confident**

 Tell an Adult

 Act Bravely & Walk Away

 Notice Surroundings

 Display Kindness

Discuss how to apply the story...

1. Do you think your friends would help you **STAND** against bullying?

2. What can you do to encourage your friends to **STAND** together against bullying?

3. Has there been a time when you saw someone who was being bullied? What happened?

4. Were there other people around? What did they do?

5. Even though Charlie stopped, why was it important for Leo and his friends to tell an adult?

FOR PARENTS & MENTORS: *If your child has been the victim of bullying in the past, understand that it may take a lot of courage to stand up for others. Ignoring bullying behavior is never a good option because it is not only bad for the victim and the bully, but also for children who witness it. Reporting bullying behavior to an adult is very important for kids to do. Help your child see that telling an adult about bullying is not "tattling," but a way to prevent further bullying from happening. Teachers, counselors and other adults can further help the victim and the bully.*

For additional tips and reference information, visit www.realMVPkids.com.

Meet the

mvpkids®

featured in
STAND Together Against Bullying™
with their families

LUCAS MILLER

LEBRON MILLER

FAITH JORDAN

OLIVIA WAGNER

LEO RUSSO

FRANKIE RUSSO

CLAUDIA RUSSO
Mother

EZEKIEL JORDAN

BLAKE JAMES

mvpkids ®

STAND against bullying!

Will YOU take a STAND to stop bullying?

Stand in front of a mirror and say the pledge aloud, then share with someone how you've decided to STAND against bullying.

Use this QR code for a download of the STAND pledge to sign and display!

I pledge to take a

S.T.A.N.D.

when faced with any bullying situation.

I promise that I will strive to...

 Stand tall and be confident.

 Tell an adult if I run into trouble.

 Act bravely and walk away if I need to.

 Notice what is going on around me.

 Display kindness to others.

In a study conducted by StopBullying.gov, "about 49% of children in grades 4–12 reported being bullied by other students at school at least once during the past month, whereas 30.8% reported bullying others during that time."[1] From a very young age, we need to help our children understand and **STAND** against bullying.

———————

Do you need more resources and help regarding bullying? Please visit our website at

www.realMVPkids.com/stand-against-bullying/

The U.S. official government website can be found at

www.stopbullying.gov/

[1] *"Facts About Bullying." StopBullying.gov, www.stopbullying.gov/media/facts/index.html.*

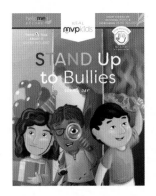

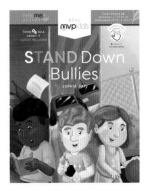